GDB
1/24/14

A Guide to
AMERICAN STATES

Illinois

THE PRAIRIE STATE

MEDIA ENHANCED BOOKS
AV2 BY WEIGL
ADDED VALUE · AUDIO VISUAL

www.av2books.com

AV² provides enriched content that supplements and complements this book. Weigl's AV² books strive to create inspired learning and engage young minds in a total learning experience.

Your AV² Media Enhanced books come alive with...

Audio
Listen to sections of the book read aloud.

Key Words
Study vocabulary, and complete a matching word activity.

Video
Watch informative video clips.

Quizzes
Test your knowledge.

Go to www.av2books.com, and enter this book's unique code.

BOOK CODE

Q 2 6 4 4 4 2

Embedded Weblinks
Gain additional information for research.

Slide Show
View images and captions, and prepare a presentation.

AV² by Weigl brings you media enhanced books that support active learning.

Try This!
Complete activities and hands-on experiments.

... and much, much more!

Published by AV² by Weigl
350 5th Avenue, 59th Floor
New York, NY 10118
Website: www.av2books.com   www.weigl.com

Library of Congress Cataloging-in-Publication Data

Craats, Rennay.
 Illinois / Rennay Craats.
    p. cm. -- (A guide to American states)
 Includes index.
 ISBN 978-1-61690-785-3 (hardcover : alk. paper) -- ISBN 978-1-61690-461-6 (online)
 1. Illinois--Juvenile literature. I. Title.
 F541.3.C73 2011
 977.3--dc23
                         2011018326

Printed in the United States of America in North Mankato, Minnesota

052011
WEP180511

Project Coordinator Jordan McGill
Art Director Terry Paulhus

Photo Credits
Every reasonable effort has been made to trace ownership and to obtain permission to reprint copyright material. The publishers would be pleased to have any errors or omissions brought to their attention so that they may be corrected in subsequent printings.

Weigl acknowledges Getty Images as its primary image supplier for this title.
Photo of Abraham Lincoln Presidential Library and Museum on page 20 courtesy of Edward A. Thomas.

Contents

Navy Pier and the Chicago skyline are among the sights most familiar to people who visit the state of Illinois.

Introduction

Near the center of the United States lies Illinois, a state renowned for its farms and factories as well as the glittering city of Chicago. Located in the northeast corner of the state, Chicago is the third-largest city in the country and a national leader in finance and technology. Walking along its busy streets, it is difficult to imagine the prairies that covered the land just a few hundred years ago. Back then, prairies stretched as far as the eye could see, earning Illinois its official nickname, the Prairie State. Illinois is often also referred to as the Land of Lincoln, which is the state slogan.

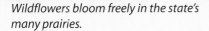
Wildflowers bloom freely in the state's many prairies.

The Chicago Board of Trade is an important place. Deals are made there involving agricultural and financial contracts.

The early pioneers who settled in Illinois built a successful farm-based economy. While agriculture remains important in the state, Illinois is now home to a wide range of industries. From commerce and trade to digital technology and health care, Illinois is forging ahead with the pioneer spirit of its founders.

Chicago is often referred to as the Windy City. Historians say that the boasting and bragging of local politicians earned Chicago the nickname, but many people who have felt the biting winter wind, which is called "the hawk," think otherwise. Chicago is one of the most diverse places in the nation. People from more than 100 ethnic groups call the city home and bring to Illinois a wide range of customs, traditional foods, and cultural interests, notably in music. Chicago's various annual music festivals bring energy and excitement to the city.

Where Is Illinois?

Illinois is located near the center of the United States in a region called the Midwest. It has the largest population of any Midwestern state, with the vast majority of the state's population living in the Chicago area. Yet Illinois is more than just Chicago. The state also boasts many farms, small towns, rolling hills, and flat prairies.

In autumn, the colors of the season are shown in the trees at Pere Marquette State Park, which is the largest state park in Illinois.

Although it is called the Prairie State, prairies are not the only type of terrain in Illinois. Thick forests, soaring cliffs, and sparkling lakes are found in some areas. However, Illinois's many factories and farms have damaged the once-**pristine** environment. Beginning in the late twentieth century, the state introduced strong measures aimed at controlling pollution and environmental waste. In 1995, the state government implemented Conservation 2000, a program to conserve, restore, and manage state parks and natural resources. The program, which was later renamed Partners for Conservation and extended to the year 2021, also regulates hunting and fishing to keep animal populations at **sustainable** levels. Biologists have identified **endangered species**, and efforts are being made to save them. Many Illinois residents do their part for the environment by saving grass clippings and leaves for **composting** rather than burning them. In addition, many areas recycle and reuse paper, plastic, glass, and metal.

Amazing rock formations were created millions of years ago at Garden of the Gods in Shawnee National Forest.

Mapping Illinois

Three rivers and five states border Illinois. The Mississippi River separates Illinois from Iowa and Missouri to the west. The Ohio River separates southeastern Illinois from Kentucky. The Wabash River forms part of the state's border with Indiana, which lies to the east. The far northeastern part of Illinois is bordered by part of Lake Michigan. Wisconsin forms the northern border.

Sites and Symbols

STATE SEAL
Illinois

STATE BIRD
Cardinal

STATE FLOWER
Violet

STATE FLAG
Illinois

STATE ANIMAL
White-tailed Deer

STATE TREE
White Oak

Nickname The Prairie State

Motto State Sovereignty, National Union

Song "Illinois," words by Charles H. Chamberlain and music by Archibald Johnston

Entered the Union December 3, 1818, as the 21st state

Capital Springfield

Population (2010 Census) 12,830,632 Ranked 5th state

STATE CAPITAL

Springfield is the capital of Illinois. Abraham Lincoln lived in Springfield from 1837 to 1861, when he moved to the White House in Washington, D.C., as president.

United States

Hawai'i   Alaska

Illinois

LEGEND

——	Road
——	River
⭐	State Capital
●	City
▬	Illinois
——	State Border

N

Map Scale

0   50 Miles

The Land

Illinois has four major land regions. They are the Central Lowland, the Ozark Plateaus, the Interior Low Plateaus, and the Coastal Plain. The Central Lowland covers about 90 percent of the state. The **glaciers** that moved across the land during the last Ice Age created this region's rolling plains and rich soil. The Central Lowland area is divided into a number of subregions, including the Driftless Plains, the Till Plains, and the Great Lakes Plains. The Ozark Plateaus, the second major land region, are found along the Mississippi River in the southwest. The Interior Low Plateaus, or Shawnee Hills, sprawl across much of the southern part of Illinois. The hills range from about 325 feet to 1,064 feet above sea level and feature bluffs, valleys, and forests. The Coastal Plain at the southern tip of Illinois is hilly toward the north and flat in the south.

Illinois has approximately 500 rivers and streams. Most of them flow into the mighty Mississippi River, on the state's western border. Illinois's rivers, streams, and lakes provide drinking water for the state's citizens, as well as a means of transportation.

COASTAL PLAIN

Illinois's Coastal Plain region is generally flat, with very productive land.

CENTRAL LOWLAND

The Central Lowland contains such geographic features as shallow river valleys and fertile plains.

INTERIOR LOW PLATEAUS

The Interior Low Plateaus contain the Shawnee Hills, which are covered with forestland.

OZARK PLATEAUS

Horseshoe Lake is located in a low flood plain that follows the Mississippi River down to the state's border with Kentucky.

I DIDN'T KNOW THAT!

The state of Illinois has a land area of 55,584 square miles. It ranks 25th in size in the country.

The Illinois River is the largest river that is completely within the state's borders.

At one time, the Chicago River flowed eastward into Lake Michigan. In the late nineteenth century, a series of locks were built that changed the river's direction. It now flows westward toward the Mississippi River.

The highest point in the state is Charles Mound near the Wisconsin border. It is 1,235 feet high.

An early Chicagoan once described the city's winds as being "strong enough to strip the fur off a buffalo."

Severe and dangerous thunderstorms are common in Illinois, especially during the springtime months.

Climate

Illinois has cold, snowy winters and hot, wet summers. In summer, the average temperature is about 75° Fahrenheit. Winter temperatures average around 30° F, though they can plunge below freezing for weeks at a time. The southern part of the state is typically warmer than the north. The hottest recorded temperature in Illinois was 117° F, on July 14, 1954, in East St. Louis. The coldest was −36° F, on January 5, 1999, in Congerville. Illinois gets an average of about 39 inches of precipitation each year. Severe thunderstorms and deadly tornadoes can occur. In winter snowstorms are common, and heavy snow can fall.

Average Annual Temperature Across Illinois

The average annual temperature varies for different cities across Illinois. Which city in the graph here has the highest average temperature? Which city has the lowest average temperature? Why might the average temperature be so different in the city that has the highest average temperature and the city that has the lowest average temperature?

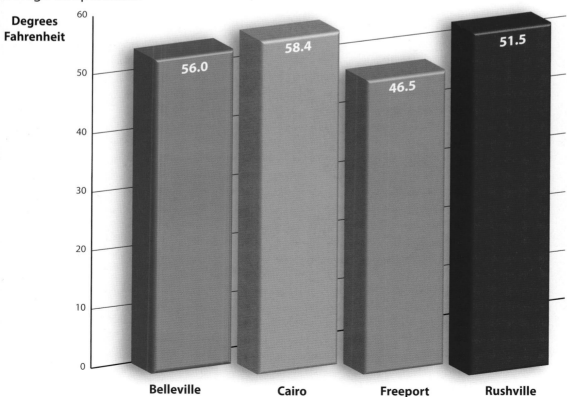

Natural Resources

Illinois is rich in natural resources. Oil and coal are the two most commercially important minerals found in Illinois. Most of the state's oil fields are spread across the southeastern region. Although **reserves** are large, oil supplies less than 1 percent of the state's electrical power. Nuclear power and coal-fired plants provide more than 90 percent of the state's electricity, and most of the rest comes from natural gas.

Coal is one of the most important minerals found in Illinois, and many people in the state work in coal-mining.

Illinois is one of the leading producers of bituminous coal in the United States. This type of coal is found in basinlike landforms in the central and southern parts of the state. Coal is mined in 11 counties in Illinois. Although there are enormous reserves of coal, demand for it is lower now than it was in the first half of the 1900s. This is partly because when coal is burned, it produces a great deal of sulfur, carbon dioxide, and other gases that contribute to air pollution and other problems.

Tripoli, which is a rock that contains tiny bits of quartz, and industrial sand are also produced in Illinois. The town of Galena, in western Illinois, once produced 85 percent of the lead in the United States.

The first oil wells in Illinois were drilled in 1853. Today, there are more than 30,000 oil and gas production wells in the state.

Bituminous coal is soft coal with a high energy value that is found in about two-thirds of the state. Each year, about 32 million tons of coal are mined in Illinois.

Coal was discovered in Illinois more than 300 years ago. It was first mined in the state about 200 years ago.

The light, spongy material called peat is the first stage in the formation of coal. When burned, peat can be used for heating purposes. Illinois's peat deposits are found in lakes and swamps in the state's northeast.

Limestone and dolomite are the rocks that are most widely dug up in Illinois. Crushed stone, which is used for construction and road surfacing, is the state's most important rock product.

Plants

Before the early settlers arrived, most of what is now northern and central Illinois was covered with tall-grass prairie, and southern Illinois was thick with woodlands. Although much of the land has been cleared for agriculture and industry, the state retains many beautiful natural areas. Today, woodlands and forests cover about 6,400 square miles of Illinois. The state's forests are filled mostly with hardwood trees such as black walnut, maple, and oak. Other common trees include sycamore, mulberry, black cherry, ash, pine, dogwood, and hackberry.

The state's official flower is the violet. This delicate purple flower is found all over Illinois, most commonly in meadows and forests. Many other wildflowers are found in the state. Tall, graceful black-eyed Susans flourish along roadsides, buttercups spread across the grasses, and goldenrod and bluebells bloom almost everywhere.

BLACK WALNUT TREE

Black walnut trees are among the many types of hardwood trees found in the state.

VIOLETS

There are hundreds of types of violets found around the world. While purple is the most common color, violets can also be blue, yellow, or white.

BLACK-EYED SUSANS

Black-eyed Susans are found in all counties of Illinois. They can grow to more than 2 feet tall.

PRAIRIE BLAZING STARS

This common wildflower, which is said to resemble a fairy's wand, is often found in prairies and meadows. It can grow to 5 feet tall.

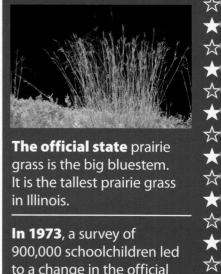

The official state prairie grass is the big bluestem. It is the tallest prairie grass in Illinois.

In 1973, a survey of 900,000 schoolchildren led to a change in the official state tree. It was changed from the native oak to the white oak.

In 2007, scientists discovered a fossilized rain forest in a coal mine near Danville in eastern Illinois. The forest, which was probably buried during an earthquake, contained trees, mosses, shrubs, and tall ferns.

The Shawnee National Forest in the southern part of the state is the only national forest in Illinois. Among its trees are maple, dogwood, oak, and beech.

Animals

Various mammal species can be found in Illinois. Muskrats, minks, and beavers are found near rivers and lakes. Woodchucks, opossums, skunks, deer, foxes, and coyotes inhabit wooded areas. Squirrels and raccoons are common both in the forests and in urban and suburban areas.

Birdlife in Illinois is exceptionally diverse, from the common robins and pigeons to the elusive red-tailed hawks and Eastern screech owls. Some species, such as the purple finch and redheaded woodpecker, are permanent residents. Others, such as the turkey vulture and indigo bunting, are seasonal visitors. Part of Illinois sits along the Mississippi Flyway, one of the most important routes for **migratory** birds. This means that a wealth of bird species pass through the state's skies and natural areas when they travel elsewhere.

Many different kinds of fish inhabit Illinois's streams, lakes, and rivers, though water pollution has reduced some populations. Bass, carp, catfish, trout, and pike are among the most common sportfishing species.

RED FOX

Red foxes can be found in urban areas as well as around forests, in grasslands, and in agricultural regions. They can run up to 30 miles per hour.

BLUEGILL

The bluegill was adopted as the state fish in 1986. A member of the sunfish family, it is found throughout the state, mostly in clear lakes.

RACCOON

The number of raccoons in the state has increased dramatically. Scientists think there are more in Illinois today than there were when the first European settlers arrived.

REDHEADED WOODPECKER

Redheaded woodpeckers have become more scarce in Illinois, in part because their habitat is threatened. Their diet includes insects, seeds, nuts, and corn.

The state animal is the white-tailed deer. This graceful animal, which is native to Illinois, was once almost wiped out in the state.

A large influx of settlers in the early 1800s led to a great increase in hunting. As a result, by about 1830 many once-common large mammal species had vanished, including bison, mountain lions, and elk.

Endangered animal species in Illinois include the gray bat, piping plover, and pallid sturgeon.

A three-day festival called Bald Eagle Days is celebrated in January in Rock Island. People gather to watch eagles migrate south along the Mississippi River.

Tourism

A popular tourist destination, Illinois is one of the 10 most-visited states in the country. Chicago's parks, festivals, and museums are key attractions. The Field Museum displays collections from the World's Columbian Exposition of 1893 as well as mummies, meteorities, and dinosaurs. Young tourists visiting Chicago's lakefront are enthralled by Navy Pier and its exciting playground.

To gain a sense of life in Illinois in the 1800s, visitors can head to Galena, a former mining town on the banks of the Mississippi River. From its charming downtown to the home of President Ulysses S. Grant, Galena offers a feast of architecture and history blended with art galleries, shopping, and other attractions.

The memory of another historical figure, Abraham Lincoln, draws many visitors to Springfield. The Abraham Lincoln Presidential Library and Museum opened in 2005, featuring state-of-the-art exhibits about the president's life and times.

CHICAGO

Important architects designed many of Chicago's notable structures. Visitors enjoy taking tours to explore the city and its buildings.

ABRAHAM LINCOLN PRESIDENTIAL LIBRARY AND MUSEUM

In addition to the Abraham Lincoln Presidential Library and Museum, tourists in Springfield can visit many other sites devoted to the 16th president, including his home, law offices, and tomb.

FIELD MUSEUM

Sue, a dinosaur skeleton, is one of the most popular exhibits at the Field Museum. It is one of the world's largest, most complete *Tyrannosaurus Rex* fossils ever discovered.

NAVY PIER

Chicago's Navy Pier features a children's museum, theaters, an indoor ice-skating rink, a miniature golf course, and a 150-foot-high Ferris wheel that provides a stunning view of the city's skyline.

I DIDN'T KNOW THAT!

Every summer, people flock to the Taste of Chicago, a 10-day festival of food and music on the city's lakefront.

The Museum of Science and Industry in Chicago, which contains more than 35,000 artifacts, draws more than 1.5 million visitors each year.

The Art Institute of Chicago was founded in 1879. It houses some of the world's greatest Impressionist paintings, as well as collections of modern art, African art, and armor.

Industry

Illinois's farming past led to some amazing agricultural developments. Blacksmith William Parlin settled in Illinois in 1840 and began manufacturing plows soon after. He helped develop many devices, such as stalk cutters and double plows, that eased the difficult work of the farmer.

Industries in Illinois
Value of Goods and Services in Millions of Dollars

While Illinois has a significant manufacturing industry, the state makes most of its money from finance, insurance, and real estate and from information and professional services. What sector contributes the least amount of money to the state? Why might this be the case?

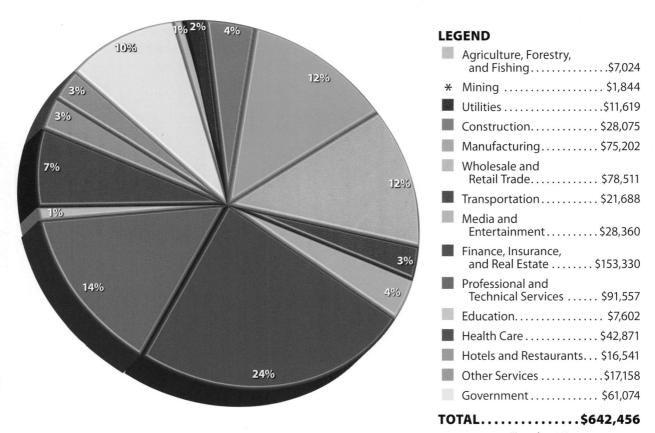

LEGEND

	Agriculture, Forestry, and Fishing	$7,024
*	Mining	$1,844
	Utilities	$11,619
	Construction	$28,075
	Manufacturing	$75,202
	Wholesale and Retail Trade	$78,511
	Transportation	$21,688
	Media and Entertainment	$28,360
	Finance, Insurance, and Real Estate	$153,330
	Professional and Technical Services	$91,557
	Education	$7,602
	Health Care	$42,871
	Hotels and Restaurants	$16,541
	Other Services	$17,158
	Government	$61,074

TOTAL. $642,456

*Less than 1%.

Although fewer than 4 percent of U.S. farms are in Illinois, the state's hardworking farmers keep Illinois among the top agricultural producers in the nation. More than three-fourths of the land in Illinois is used for agriculture. Corn and soybeans are the most important crops. Illinois ranks high among the states in agricultural **exports**, especially feed grains and soybeans. Aside from crops, many farmers raise livestock. Hogs are the most important livestock in Illinois, and the state consistently ranks near the top in U.S. hog production. Cattle, calves, and dairy products are also important to the state economy.

Factories in Illinois make many kinds of tools and equipment that are exported to the rest of the world. The manufacture of farm and construction machinery is vital to the state economy. Chemicals, transportation equipment, and plastic and rubber goods also are key products made in Illinois.

The John Deere company employs many people in Illinois making farm machinery, which is colored a characteristic bright green.

Blacksmith John Deere moved to Illinois from Vermont in 1836. He invented the first successful steel plow. His invention replaced the old cast-iron plow and made farming easier and more productive throughout the Midwest.

Barbed wire was invented by Joseph Glidden of DeKalb in the 1870s. To control their herds, livestock owners needed barbed wire, which is fencing with sharp points or edges.

Illinois is one of the nation's leading producers of **ethanol**, a fuel that is made from corn.

Illinois boasts about 8,000 miles of railroad, which is more than any other state except Texas.

A McDonald's Museum in Des Plaines is built on the site of the original 1955 McDonald's restaurant.

Goods and Services

Illinois's agricultural bounty is tied to the state's importance in food processing. Many of the nation's largest food corporations are headquartered in Illinois. Food products that are made in factories across the state include sausages, dairy products, and breakfast cereals.

Technology is another key component of the Illinois economy. Computers and other electronic goods, such as wireless telephones, Internet-access products, and **embedded** electronic systems, are produced in the Chicago area. Also important is biotechnology. Several of the nation's largest manufacturers of health-care products and **pharmaceuticals** are headquartered in northern Illinois.

The Ford Motor Company has a plant in Chicago that assembles cars.

Chicago's McCormick Place hosts many conventions each year. Companies in a particular industry, such as candy and snack food, display their products at these conventions.

Doctors, lawyers, teachers, and government employees are among the part of the workforce employed in the service sector. A large portion of the service sector caters to groups and businesses that head to Chicago for the many **conventions** and trade shows that are held there each year. These meetings generate much revenue for the state and provide employment for many people in the tourism industry, such as hotel clerks and restaurant workers.

Another important part of Illinois's economy is the financial industry. The state is home to more than 2,300 commercial banks, more than 2,000 insurance companies, and many other financial service corporations. Illinois also has many warehousing and distribution facilities and has a vast transportation network, making use of its central location in the United States.

Illinois was once the broomcorn capital of the world. Broomcorn, a variety of upright grasses once used to make brooms, required about 300 people for a harvest, so many farmers switched to regular corn. There is still an annual Broom Corn Festival in Arcola.

Argonne National Laboratory, Fermilab, and the National Center for Supercomputing Applications are among the more than 70 federal research centers located in Illinois.

The Chicago Board of Trade is one of the world's top **commodity** exchanges. Each day, millions of investors trade shares of commodities such as corn, wheat, soybeans, gold, and silver.

Many travelers transfer to international flights at Chicago O'Hare International Airport.

American Indians

The first residents of Illinois, thousands of years ago, moved with the seasons to places that had available plants and animals. They were followed by other American Indians who engaged in trade with nearby groups, planted gardens, and settled in small villages. About 700 AD, they were followed by Indians who established large towns. These Indians also built mounds of earth as temples and burial grounds. They established trade relations from the Great Lakes to the Gulf of Mexico. The Mound Builders introduced corn, from Mexico, to the area and invented hoes made of flint to **till** the land. The Mound Builders also created bows and arrows for hunting. The community of Cahokia, in western Illinois, had about 20,000 people around the year 1200, making it one of the largest cities in the world at the time. During the 1500s, the number of Mound Builders decreased due to lack of food, overcrowding, and disease.

Monks Mound and other mounds in Illinois were built by Indians who established large towns hundreds of years ago. The mounds were built of soil and clay.

By the time the first European explorers arrived in the 1600s, Illinois was populated by the Illiniwek, a **confederation** of 12 independent American Indian peoples. The Illiniwek established a peaceful society based on agriculture and hunting. By the 1700s, seven of the Illiniwek peoples had migrated or merged with the other Illinois groups, leaving the Cahokia, Kaskaskia, Michigamea, Peoria, and Tamaroa as the principal tribes. Attacks by invading peoples, especially the Iroquois, killed many of the Illiniwek. By the early 1800s, the Kaskaskia and the Peoria were the only Illiniwek peoples who remained.

Shabbona was the chief of the Ottawa Indians who lived near the Kankakee River south of Chicago.

I DIDN'T KNOW THAT!

Established in 1953, the American Indian Center in Chicago is a vital educational and cultural resource for American Indians living and working in the metropolitan area.

One of the largest mounds in the United States is Monks Mound in Cahokia Mounds State Historic Site. Its base covers 14 acres, and it is 100 feet high.

Like many American Indian groups, the Illiniwek suffered numerous outbreaks of the deadly disease known as smallpox, which was carried to the New World by European explorers and settlers.

The Illiniwek played a field sport called lacrosse. They also played games of chance with straws or dice.

The religious practices of the Illiniwek involved appealing to spirits for guidance and assistance. They worshipped one god, Kitchesmanetoa, above the others.

Father Jacques Marquette was a French missionary who traveled to the Illinois region in the 1670s, where he met and established good relations with Indians.

Explorers and Missionaries

The first European explorers of the Illinois region came from France. In 1673, Louis Jolliet and a missionary, Father Jacques Marquette, traveled down the Mississippi River and then up the Illinois River. They came upon the Kaskaskia, who welcomed them.

In 1680, the French explorer René-Robert Cavelier, sieur de La Salle, entered Illinois and established Fort Crèvecoeur along the Illinois River. Two years later, he and Henri de Tonti built Fort St. Louis atop a bluff in what is now Starved Rock State Park. The fort served as a major fur-trading post for many years. Soon, settlements began to spring up.

Marquette return in 1675, starting the first Roman Catholic mission among the Kaskaskia. French priests soon established several other missions in Illinois.

Timeline of Settlement

Early Exploration

1673 Father Jacques Marquette, accompanied by Louis Jolliet, arrives in Illinois and encounters Indian groups there.

First Settlements

1680 La Salle builds Fort Crèvecoeur near present-day Peoria.

1699 French priests establish a mission at Cahokia, the oldest European settlement in Illinois.

British Rule

1763 As a result of the French and Indian War, the French give control of Illinois to the British.

American Revolution

1778 George Rogers Clark of Virginia and his men defeat the British at Kaskaskia.

1779 Jean-Baptist-Point du Sable builds a trading post along the Chicago River, at the site of what will become Chicago.

Territory and Statehood

1787 Congress passes the Northwest Ordinance, establishing the Northwest Territory, which includes Illinois.

1803 U.S. troops build Fort Dearborn on the future site of Chicago.

1809 The Illinois Territory is established.

1818 Illinois becomes a state.

Early Settlers

Stories of the friendly native Indian groups and great hunting opportunities in Illinois lured many early settlers to the area. A mission in Cahokia became the first permanent European settlement in the state. In 1703, French missionaries established the town of Kaskaskia, named after one of the local Indian groups.

Map of Settlements and Resources in Early Illinois

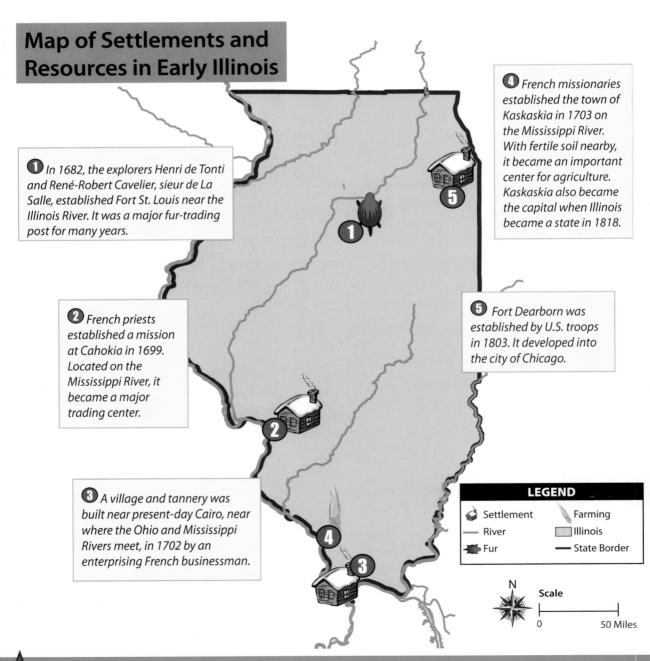

1 In 1682, the explorers Henri de Tonti and René-Robert Cavelier, sieur de La Salle, established Fort St. Louis near the Illinois River. It was a major fur-trading post for many years.

4 French missionaries established the town of Kaskaskia in 1703 on the Mississippi River. With fertile soil nearby, it became an important center for agriculture. Kaskaskia also became the capital when Illinois became a state in 1818.

2 French priests established a mission at Cahokia in 1699. Located on the Mississippi River, it became a major trading center.

5 Fort Dearborn was established by U.S. troops in 1803. It developed into the city of Chicago.

3 A village and tannery was built near present-day Cairo, near where the Ohio and Mississippi Rivers meet, in 1702 by an enterprising French businessman.

LEGEND

Settlement		Farming	
River		Illinois	
Fur		State Border	

N

Scale

0   50 Miles

Fur trading flourished as more **immigrants** arrived, attracted by the massive herds of bison roaming the area. More forts and settlements were soon established.

The British saw the fur-trading value of the Illinois region and soon challenged the French for control, in the French and Indian War. The British defeated the French in 1763. Many French settlers and Indians, unhappy with the transfer of power, left Illinois.

After the American Revolution, settlement in Illinois increased. Most settlers chose to build their homes in the south. The first settlement in northern Illinois, built around Fort Dearborn, developed into the city of Chicago. Treaties with the Indians made more land available to settlers. Many Indians were not content with the terms of the treaties, however. When war broke out between the United States and Britain in 1812, many Indian groups supported Britain in the hopes that they would have their land returned.

The United States won the war, however, and increasing numbers of settlers began to arrive from the East. Between 1818, when Illinois became a state, and 1830, the population of Illinois more than quadrupled.

The city of Chicago developed in the early 1800s at a place where Indians and white settlers engaged in fur trading.

I DIDN'T KNOW THAT!

The French built Fort de Chartres and Fort Kaskaskia, which became important government and military centers.

The fur trade that began in the late 1600s made Illinois commercially important.

Charles Juchereau de St. Denis built a village and tannery near the Ohio River in southern Illinois in 1702.

Jean-Baptist-Point du Sable was Chicago's first settler. A fur trader of French- African descent, he built a successful trading post along the Chicago River in 1779.

In 1787, Congress passed an act providing for the organization of the Northwest Territory, which included Illinois. In 1800, Illinois was included in the Indiana Territory. Nine years later, Illinois became its own territory.

When Illinois became a state in 1818, it had a population of only 35,000. By 1830, the population had topped 157,000.

Notable People

Many notable Illinoisans contributed to development of their state and country. President Ronald Reagan was born in Illinois, and three other presidents lived in the state before becoming president. They were Abraham Lincoln, Ulysses S. Grant, and Barack Obama. In addition, a number of social reformers have come from the Prairie State. In recent times, Hillary Rodham Clinton, who was born in Chicago and grew up in Park Ridge, served as the First Lady of the United States when her husband, Bill Clinton, was president. She became secretary of state in 2009.

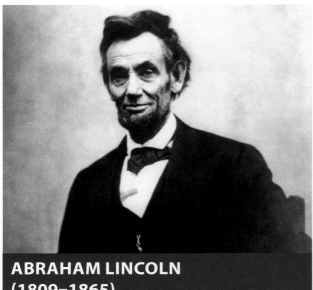

ABRAHAM LINCOLN (1809–1865)

Abraham Lincoln settled in Illinois when he was 21. He studied law and served in the state legislature. During an unsuccessful bid for a U.S. Senate seat in 1858, he engaged in a series of debates with Stephen Douglas. Lincoln argued that slavery should not be allowed in new states. Lincoln was elected president in 1860, and the Civil War began the next year. The new president faced the difficult task of keeping the Union together, guiding the nation through the war, and attempting to end slavery. He was **assassinated** in April 1865.

RONALD REAGAN (1911–2004)

Ronald Reagan was born in Tampico and grew up in Dixon. After graduating from Eureka College, he became a radio broadcaster. He moved to California in 1937 to become an actor. Reagan appeared in a number of movies and became involved in politics after serving as president of a major actor's **union**. He was elected governor of California in 1966 and served two terms. In 1980, he was elected president of the United States. During his two terms in office, he cut taxes, increased military spending, and improved relations with the Soviet Union.

JANE ADDAMS (1860–1935)

Jane Addams was born in Cedarville. While traveling in Europe, she visited a **settlement house** and decided to open a similar institution for the poor in Chicago. Hull House, which opened in 1889, was one of the first settlement houses in the United States, providing aid, food, and education for thousands of people.

HAROLD WASHINGTON (1922–1987)

Harold Washington was born in Chicago. He grew up there, graduated from Roosevelt University, and received a law degree from Northwestern University. Washington served in the Illinois state legislature and then in the U.S. House of Representatives. In 1983, he was elected as the first African-American mayor of Chicago. He worked to reform Chicago's government and politics.

BARACK OBAMA (1961–)

Barack Obama was born in Honolulu, Hawaii. After graduating from law school in 1991, he worked in Chicago. In 1996, he was elected to the Illinois Senate. Eight years later, he was elected to the U.S. Senate. In 2009, he became the 44th U.S. president, the first African American to hold the position.

I DIDN'T KNOW THAT!

Betty Friedan (1921–2006), a native of Peoria, wrote *The Feminine Mystique* in 1963. The book launched the modern feminist movement of the late twentieth century. She was also the first president of the National Organization for Women.

Richard J. Daley (1902–1976) was the mayor of Chicago for 21 years, from 1955 until he died. He was one of the most powerful politicians in the Democratic Party and in the United States. One of his sons, Richard M. Daley, was elected mayor in 1989 and served until 2011.

Population

More than 12.8 million people live in Illinois, making it one of the most populous states in the country. Most Illinoisans live in cities and towns. Fewer than 15 percent live in rural areas. Much of the Prairie State's population is centered in and around Chicago, which has a population of more than 2.8 million residents. Almost one-fourth of the state's people live in Chicago. If you include surrounding suburbs and smaller cities, the population of the Chicago metropolitan area soars to 9.8 million. With the exception of Springfield, which lies near the center of the state, most of the state's largest cities are located in northern Illinois. Several, such as Aurora, Naperville, Elgin, and Cicero, are part of the Chicago metropolitan area.

Illinois Population 1950–2010

The population of Illinois has grown steadily in the past 60 years. What are the different factors that contribute to a state's population growth?

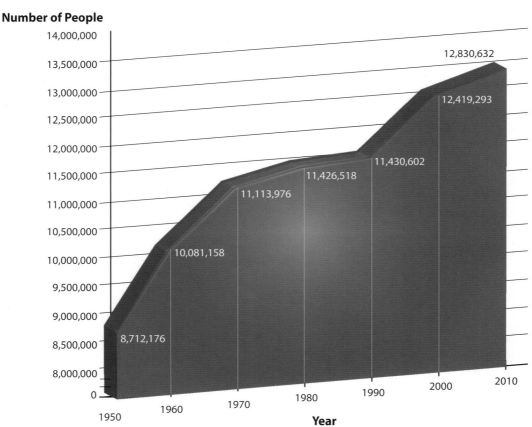

Number of People

Year	Number of People
1950	8,712,176
1960	10,081,158
1970	11,113,976
1980	11,426,518
1990	11,430,602
2000	12,419,293
2010	12,830,632

Year

Hispanic people make up a large number of new immigrants to Illinois, especially Chicago.

Although the vast majority of Illinoisans were born in the United States, the state's immigrant population began to increase greatly in the 1990s. Today, almost half of these newcomers come from Latin America, especially Mexico. Large numbers of new immigrants also come from Asia, especially China and the Philippines. Many European immigrants in past years were Poles, many of whom settled in and around Chicago. People of German, English, Irish, and Italian ancestry also have a long history as residents of Illinois. About 15 percent of Illinois's people are African American. American Indians, though once numerous in the region, now make up less than 1 percent of Illinois's population.

Illinois still has many small towns, such as Chatsworth, whose Main Streets look much as they did years ago.

I DIDN'T KNOW THAT!

Illinois residents seeking higher education can choose from 12 public colleges and universities and many more private colleges and universities across the state.

The University of Chicago, one of the most intellectually challenging schools in the United States, was founded in 1890.

Because Superman's fictional home was Metropolis, the citizens of the southern Illinois city bearing the same name claim the superhero as one of their own. His image can be seen throughout the city.

Politics and Government

Illinois joined the Union on December 3, 1818. The state adopted its first constitution that year. New constitutions were adopted in 1848, 1870, and 1970. Illinois's government, like the federal government, is made up of three branches. They are the executive, the legislative, and the judicial branches.

Construction on the Illinois state capitol building in Springfield began in 1868. It took 20 years to complete work on the building.

The executive branch is headed by the governor, who is elected for a four-year term. The governor appoints officials, sets budgets, and has the authority to **veto** bills passed by the legislature. The legislative branch is the state legislature, which is called the General Assembly. The legislature has two parts. The Senate has 59 members, and the House of Representatives has 118 members. Senators are elected to either a two-year or a four-year term. Representatives serve two-year terms. The legislative branch passes new laws and changes existing ones. The judicial branch consists of the state's courts. The state's highest court is the Illinois Supreme Court, with seven justices who are elected to 10-year terms. There are also lower-level courts in the state.

Illinois has three levels of local government. They are county, township, and municipal government. Most of Illinois's 102 counties are divided into townships.

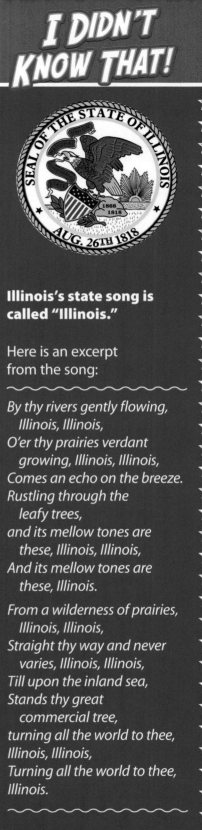

I DIDN'T KNOW THAT!

Illinois's state song is called "Illinois."

Here is an excerpt from the song:

By thy rivers gently flowing,
Illinois, Illinois,
O'er thy prairies verdant
growing, Illinois, Illinois,
Comes an echo on the breeze.
Rustling through the
leafy trees,
and its mellow tones are
these, Illinois, Illinois,
And its mellow tones are
these, Illinois.

From a wilderness of prairies,
Illinois, Illinois,
Straight thy way and never
varies, Illinois, Illinois,
Till upon the inland sea,
Stands thy great
commercial tree,
turning all the world to thee,
Illinois, Illinois,
Turning all the world to thee,
Illinois.

Barack Obama was a U.S. senator from Illinois when he was elected president of the United States.

Cultural Groups

With so many different ethnic groups and heritages, Illinois has a rich mix of cultures. People from nearly every country in the world live in Illinois. Chicago is one of the most ethnically diverse cities in the United States.

Illinois has a large Hispanic-American population, which is concentrated in the Chicago area. To celebrate their culture, many Mexican Americans take part in the Fiesta del Sol in Chicago. It is one of the largest Mexican festivals in the nation. Illinois also has welcomed many immigrants from Southeast Asia, especially from Thailand, the Philippines, and Vietnam.

African Americans have contributed greatly to the cultural richness of Illinois. During the first half of the 1900s, many African Americans left the Southern states in search of greater freedom and work in the North. By 1918, some 60,000 African Americans called Chicago home. By 1950, that number had risen to nearly 500,000, and by 1970, it had surpassed 1 million. Today, African Americans make up 15 percent of Illinoisans and 35 percent of Chicagoans.

The Chicago Jazz Festival has been held for more than 30 years. The festival has featured such stars as saxophone player Sonny Rollins.

Each year, before St. Patrick's Day, workers dye the Chicago River green.

African American culture blossomed in Chicago in the early to mid-1900s, especially the jazz and blues music scene. Many New Orleans musicians, including jazz great Louis Armstrong, came to Chicago. So began the Chicago style of jazz. The Chicago style of blues emerged with musicians such as Muddy Waters and Howlin' Wolf. They added electric instruments to the acoustic Southern blues style and gave their music a loud beat.

Illinoisans from other backgrounds celebrate their heritage in a variety of ways. Jordbruksdagarna, or Agricultural Days, is a traditional Swedish harvest festival held every September in Bishop Hill, a community in west-central Illinois. People can experience traditional Swedish music, games, and food. The Irish community paints Chicago green during the annual St. Patrick's Day festivities. The Polish community keeps its culture alive through traditional dances and museums that showcase its history and culture.

Arts and Entertainment

I llinois is a hub of arts and entertainment. Many talented children's writers have come from the state. For example, Shel Silverstein, a Chicago native, wrote and illustrated many books, including *A Light in the Attic* and *The Giving Tree*. Adults have enjoyed Illinois's talented writers, too. Ernest Hemingway was one of the state's most notable authors. In 1954, he won the Nobel Prize for Literature. His novels and short stories earned him a reputation as one of the greatest writers of the twentieth century. The poet Carl Sandburg was also born in Illinois.

Oprah Winfrey moved to Chicago in 1983. She launched her own cable and satellite network, called OWN, in 2011.

Actress Betty White is an Illinois native. She worked in radio during the 1940s, then went on to star in many television shows.

Music is a strong part of Illinois's culture. Several opera groups have entertained audiences since the early 1900s, and choirs and orchestras showcase talented musicians and singers. Jazz, blues, and folk music have also developed in the state. Blues musicians flocked to Chicago in the early 1920s, and the city has been a blues capital ever since. The annual Chicago Blues Festival attracts blues lovers and musicians from across the country.

Numerous talented actors, comedians, and television personalities are from Illinois. Comedian and actor Robin Williams was born in Chicago. He became extremely popular for his energetic style of comedy as well as his dramatic acting abilities. Bill Murray, the star of such movies as *Caddyshack*, *Ghostbusters*, and *Groundhog Day*, was born in Wilmette, a suburb north of Chicago. Hollywood star Harrison Ford was born in Chicago and raised in Park Ridge. His roles in the *Star Wars* movies and the *Indiana Jones* series ignited his acting career. Since then, he has starred in many movies, including *The Fugitive* (filmed partly in Illinois) and *Air Force One*.

Jane Lynch, the star of the TV show *Glee* and many movies, was born and raised in Dolton. Betty White, who has been a popular entertainer for many years, was born in Oak Park. Among younger entertainers, Johnny Galecki, one of the stars of *The Big Bang Theory*, was born in Belgium and moved to Chicago when he was three. Keke Palmer, of the Nickelodeon series *True Jackson, VP*, hails from Harvey.

When Oprah Winfrey talks, people listen. In 2009, it was announced that *The Oprah Winfrey Show*, which made Winfrey one of the most popular women in the nation, would end its run after 25 years in 2011. Although Winfrey was born in Mississippi, she has lived and worked in Chicago for most of her adult life.

I DIDN'T KNOW THAT!

Gwendolyn Brooks, who was raised in Chicago, was the first African-American poet to win a Pulitzer Prize for poetry. She became Illinois's **poet laureate** in 1968.

Miles Davis, born in Alton, was one of the most famous jazz trumpeters in the world.

In a way, Mickey Mouse and Goofy were born in Illinois. Their creator, Walt Disney, was born in Chicago and studied art in the city.

The Ferris wheel was invented in Illinois by George Ferris. The first model was 264 feet high. It was used for the World's Columbian Exposition in Chicago in 1893.

Sports

It is easy to stay active in Illinois. Throughout the state, there are many lakes and rivers that are ideal for swimming, fishing, and boating. Illinoisans can also bike and hike in the hills and valleys of the state's many parks.

There is no shortage of professional sports in Illinois. The Chicago Bulls dominated the National Basketball Association (NBA) during the 1990s, winning six championships. In 1998, the Bulls lost many of their big-name stars, including Michael Jordan. Still, loyal fans continue to cheer for the team.

Chicago has two major league baseball teams. The Chicago Cubs, who pack fans into Wrigley Field, won the World Series in 1907 and 1908. The Chicago White Sox, who play in U.S. Cellular Field, won the World Series in 1906, 1917, and 2005. Illinois also was the birthplace of women's baseball. During World War II, Philip Wrigley, owner of the Chicago Cubs and the Wrigley chewing gum company, started the All-American Girls Professional Baseball League. Wrigley wanted to keep baseball fans coming to games even though many male players had been sent overseas to fight in the war. The female players amazed fans with their skills.

Hiking in one of Illinois's many state parks and recreation areas is a popular pastime. Illinoisans also go rafting, canoeing, and camping throughout the state.

Football fans look to the Chicago Bears for exciting action. The Bears won the Super Bowl in 1986. In 1997, the Bears became the first team in National Football League history to win 600 games. The Bears promise high-energy athletics and a loud response at Soldier Field.

Chicago athletes also take to the ice. The Chicago Blackhawks joined the National Hockey League in 1926. Over the years, Blackhawk heroes such as Phil Esposito and Bobby Hull made hockey an important Chicago pastime. The Blackhawks won the Stanley Cup in 1934, 1936, and 1961. They won again in 2010. That year, the team was led by some exciting young stars, including center Jonathan Toews and right-winger Patrick Kane. Both players joined the team in 2007.

Jonathan Toews, one of the most popular young players on the Chicago Blackhawks, helped bring the Stanley Cup to Chicago in 2010.

National Averages Comparison

The United States is a federal republic, consisting of fifty states and the District of Columbia. Alaska and Hawai'i are the only non-contiguous, or non-touching, states in the nation. Today, the United States of America is the third-largest country in the world in population. The United States Census Bureau takes a census, or count of all the people, every ten years. It also regularly collects other kinds of data about the population and the economy. How does Illinois compare to the national average?

Comparison Chart

United States 2010 Census Data *	USA	Illinois
Admission to Union	NA	December 3, 1818
Land Area (in square miles)	3,537,438.44	55,583.58
Population Total	308,745,538	12,830,632
Population Density (people per square mile)	87.28	230.83
Population Percentage Change (April 1, 2000, to April 1, 2010)	9.7%	3.30%
White Persons (percent)	72.4%	71.5%
Black Persons (percent)	12.6%	14.5%
American Indian and Alaska Native Persons (percent)	0.9%	0.3%
Asian Persons (percent)	4.8%	4.6%
Native Hawaiian and Other Pacific Islander Persons (percent)	0.2%	—
Some Other Race (percent)	6.2%	6.7%
Persons Reporting Two or More Races (percent)	2.9%	2.3%
Persons of Hispanic or Latino Origin (percent)	16.3%	15.8%
Not of Hispanic or Latino Origin (percent)	83.7%	84.2%
Median Household Income	$52,029	$56,230
Percentage of People Age 25 or Over Who Have Graduated from High School	80.4%	81.4%

*All figures are based on the 2010 United States Census, with the exception of the last two items. Percentages may not add to 100 because of rounding.

How to Improve My Community

Strong communities make strong states. Think about what features are important in your community. What do you value? Education? Health? Forests? Safety? Beautiful spaces? Government works to help citizens create ideal living conditions that are fair to all by providing services in communities. Consider what changes you could make in your community. How would they improve your state as a whole? Using this concept web as a guide, write a report that outlines the features you think are most important in your community and what improvements could be made. A strong state needs strong communities.

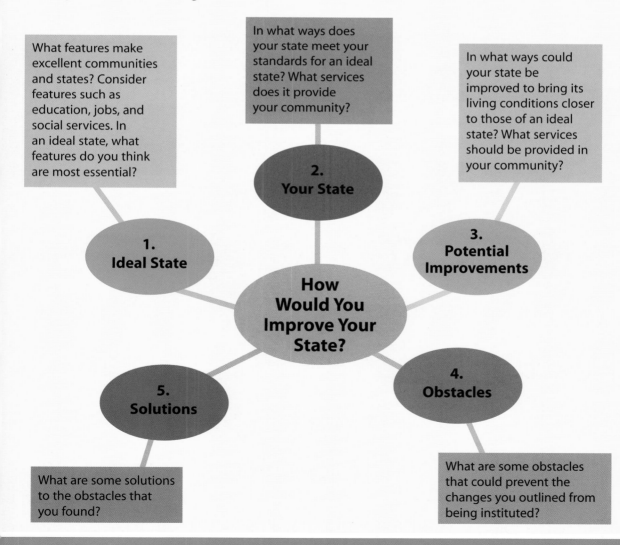

What features make excellent communities and states? Consider features such as education, jobs, and social services. In an ideal state, what features do you think are most essential?

In what ways does your state meet your standards for an ideal state? What services does it provide your community?

In what ways could your state be improved to bring its living conditions closer to those of an ideal state? What services should be provided in your community?

2. Your State

3. Potential Improvements

1. Ideal State

How Would You Improve Your State?

5. Solutions

4. Obstacles

What are some solutions to the obstacles that you found?

What are some obstacles that could prevent the changes you outlined from being instituted?

Exercise Your Mind!

Think about these questions and then use your research skills to find the answers and learn more fascinating facts about Illinois. A teacher, librarian, or parent may be able to help you locate the best sources to use in your research.

1 How was Illinoisan and U.S. President Abraham Lincoln assassinated?

2 What 1919 scandal involved the Chicago White Sox?

3 How did the Illinois city of Cairo get its name?

4 How and why does the Chicago River run backwards?

5 What was blamed for the Great Chicago Fire of 1871?

6 True or False? There were pirates in Illinois.

7 What caused the Black Hawk War in 1832?

8 True or False? Fish fell from the sky in 1890.

Words to Know

assassinated: murdered, often for political reasons

commodity: a product, usually from agriculture or mining, that is bought and sold

composting: the act of gathering organic material so that it may decay

confederation: an alliance between groups for mutual assistance and protection

conventions: large meetings to discuss common issues and share knowledge

embedded: enclosed

endangered: in danger of dying out

ethanol: a form of alcohol that can be used as a fuel in automobiles

exports: goods sent to another country

glaciers: large masses of slow-moving ice

immigrants: people who move to a new country

migratory: moving from one place to another for breeding or feeding

pharmaceuticals: medicinal drugs

poet laureate: the poet officially called upon to write poems for state occasions

pristine: undamaged, pure

reserves: supplies

settlement house: a building in a poor community where services are provided for people

species: a group of animals or plants that share the same characteristics and can mate

sustainable: able to be maintained

till: to work the land in order to raise crops

union: a group of workers organized to deal collectively with employers

veto: the right to reject or block the passing of a bill or law

Index

Log on to www.av2books.com

AV² by Weigl brings you media enhanced books that support active learning. Go to www.av2books.com, and enter the special code found on page 2 of this book. You will gain access to enriched and enhanced content that supplements and complements this book. Content includes video, audio, web links, quizzes, a slide show, and activities.

Audio
Listen to sections of the book read aloud.

Video
Watch informative video clips.

Embedded Weblinks
Gain additional information for research.

Try This!
Complete activities and hands-on experiments.

WHAT'S ONLINE?

Try This!	Embedded Weblinks	Video	EXTRA FEATURES
Test your knowledge of the state in a mapping activity.	Discover more attractions in Illinois.	Watch a video introduction to Illinois.	**Audio** Listen to sections of the book read aloud.
Find out more about precipitation in your city.	Learn more about the history of the state.	Watch a video about the features of the state.	**Key Words** Study vocabulary, and complete a matching word activity.
Plan what attractions you would like to visit in the state.	Learn the full lyrics of the state song.		
Learn more about the early natural resources of the state.			**Slide Show** View images and caption and prepare a presentatio
Write a biography about a notable resident of Illinois.			
Complete an educational census activity.			**Quizzes** Test your knowledge.

AV² was built to bridge the gap between print and digital. We encourage you to tell us what you like and what you want to see in the future.

Sign up to be an AV² Ambassador at www.av2books.com/ambassador.